REDUCED TO ABUNDANCE

Copyright © 2015 by Patricia Ballentine.

All rights reserved. No part of this book may be reproduced or transmitted in any form or by electronic or mechanical means, including photocopying, recording or by any information storage and retrieval system, without the written permission of the publisher, except where permitted by law.

Manufactured in the United States of America.

Cover work by Patricia Ballentine.

First Edition

REDUCED TO ABUNDANCE

BY

PATRICIA BALLENTINE

This book is dedicated to the matriline, or mother line, within all families.
With abundant gratitude for the generations before me,
And abundant blessings upon the generations that come through me.

I change the world
And so do each of you

Reduced to Abundance is my personal story of transformation.
From Victim of Incest
To Incest Survivor

To the Responsible Creator of a life
Filled with opportunities
To love more deeply,
Live more responsively,
And soar more freely.

The journey I am sharing with you through this series of poetic essays is not intended to minimize an early childhood experience that is clearly inexcusable. I was sexually abused by a family member when I was five years old. None of the adults in the family took action to remove the perpetrator, or to protect me or other children who were abused. The responsibility to stay out of harm's way was placed upon shoulders too young to bear the load. The even greater crime was that of being molded into the next generation of secret keepers.

Incest is a plague that survives by being transmitted through generations. In my case, it was not a blood relative who sexually violated me. It was, however, my mother who made me responsible to "stay away" from my aunt's stepfather who lived on our farm. It was my mother, grandparents, aunts and uncles who allowed this man to continue to live as a member of our family. They had their own legacy as secret keepers. I was an adult long before I realized that my mother had also been assaulted as a child by a family member.

The key to stopping the spread of this plague is not found in the sexual act, but in the keeping of secrets. It is often the victim who, as an adult, becomes a survivor and then a responsible creator of a family environment where the plague is not tolerated. Thus, the pattern is broken.

I began writing what has become *Reduced to Abundance* when my mother died in 2005. It was *not* with her death I felt the freedom to break the silence. That step had been achieved years before. Rather, it was through the experience of her dying that I realized the profound impact my relentless quest for truth, healing, and wholeness had created within her. She died with fewer secrets than she carried most of her life. We shared something that transcended a need to forgive or be forgiven. We achieved a level of empathy, which allowed us to understand each other more deeply. She died knowing I loved her, and that I was authentically grateful that she was my mother.

Drama and pain are often what draws humans together. As I gathered the pieces of my life into the pages that follow, I realized that my essence was so much larger than the drama I once allowed to define me. I also realized that I could tell my story with an economy of words that were carefully chosen, deeply honest, and reflective of the abundant goodness and magic in ALL experiences of my life.

Reduced to Abundance

When all you have taken on faith
About God on High
Has been reduced
To connecting with the Divine Presence in all things.

When all you have thought
About wisdom
Has been reduced
To knowing in your bones what is real for you.

When all you have been told
About when to speak and what to say
Has been reduced
To your own authentic words.

When all you have shared
As love
Has been reduced
To integrated thoughts and feelings flowing from the heart.

When all you have manifested
From a position of power
Has been reduced
To a powerful, personal presence.

When all you have desired
From a relationship with others
Has been reduced
To the dance of the Inner Lover.

Patricia Ballentine

When all you have felt was safe
And provided shelter
Has been reduced
To essential existence.

When all you thought you knew and felt
Has been reduced
Through the flames of change and transformation.

You emerge
As the ABUNDANCE
Of YOU!

Reduced to Abundance

Like the simmering pot on my Grandmother's stove, where nothing is wasted and slowly but surely the complex mixture within is reduced to the absolutely essential texture and flavor, my life has been *Reduced to Abundance*. Once reduced, the transformation is so complete that often I am not able to distinguish the individual pieces that went into my personal blend. And yet, I know the result is abundantly flavorful, undeniably rich, and uniquely seasoned.

My grandmother was a farm wife who wasted no energy. Whether she was cooking or sewing, no scrap was too small to transform into something delicious or beautiful. Although she was a devout Baptist (I state with loving blasphemy), she and my grandfather were great magicians. They provided seemingly endless food and shelter, love and support *in the best way they knew* to an ever-changing household of children, grandchildren and great-grandchildren.

There were no material excesses in that home and, the fullness of the truth be known, many aspects of this farm life were incredibly harsh. There were physical and emotional violations that were passed from generation to generation. They were done through the holding of family secrets and repeated patterns, the turning away of eyes that saw and voices that chose not to speak. Yet her kitchen remains the place where the child within me still returns for warmth and a deep sense of safety. The blending of aromas from that simmering pot on the stove and her magical touch against my cheek would often transform my feeling of being the smallest insignificant scrap of the family into feeling like a loved ingredient of our complex family mixture. Even in this moment, I can bring that time and space forward.

Beyond the safe walls of that kitchen, violations loomed, domestic violence and sexual abuse lived and the beast in many forms was often at the door. Through the door came an ever changing blend of family members as daughters left husbands and returned to the farm with babes, and sons went to war leaving behind wives and more children. None of us were ever turned away, but in some instances the family members were the most dangerous predators.

Yet, this is not a story built upon the fiery flames of hell, damnation or judgment that were part of the Sunday preaching in the church where my grandmother played organ and where the flowers that she and my grandfather grew in their garden blessed the pulpit. The complexity of our family creates a multitude of stories that are not mine to tell.

And yet, I must tell my story.

Reduced to Abundance is about life as I have chosen to live it throughout which my spiritual beliefs become the spices that season it to my own personal taste. Frankly, I hope I leave enough white space to allow you to place your own life ingredients into *your* pot to simmer. I hope I leave freedom with the recipe so you can then season your own simmering BEing to YOUR personal spiritual taste.

In the end, it is my hope that you will also come to a similar understanding that this life is lived by your own recipe, your own choosing of what you do with the ingredients and experiences that are yours. By reducing an experience to a clear knowing of what is our personal piece, lesson, or choice, we are able to find the extraordinary moments in time when our lives are ever changed. These are the moments when we are instantaneously aware of the perfection of the journey. They are the moments that become the forever and magical ingredients of our true story of Abundance.

When all you have taken on faith
About God on High
Has been reduced
To connecting with the Divine Presence in all things.

Crown Chakra: Perception of Oneness

Dance With Darkness Daughter of Light

I was a young child of the 50's when TV was black and white like the things I was told about God and the Devil, heaven and hell, and good and bad. However at a very young age I recognized that I was living my life in a mist of being told one thing and experiencing and witnessing another. Bad things were happening, God wasn't protecting me and no one was going to hell for inflicting pain upon the children that Jesus was said to love so much. That mist became a blanket of protection and was sometimes my only means of escaping from the dysfunction of the adults around me. It revealed a place of flower companions, and the flow of an energy that danced with my imagination and brought the colors of being alive into my young consciousness. I would find images of kings and queens in the shapes of the clouds overhead, hear the music of the rain upon the tin roof, and watch the flames of the fire dance in the pot belly stove in the kitchen. These were the memories that sustained me during the years when I struggled to recall blocks of time from my childhood that had vanished. The hold of black and white rules preached in my youth was loosened with this repression of memory. A blessing, this freed me as an adult to move through the identifiable actions of an incest survivor with less guilt. It created freedom from attachment to the opinions of others, living by beliefs that labeled actions as right or wrong rather than experiences to learn and grow from.

A fond memory as I was growing up was of my mother telling how my grandfather would occasionally wake her early on Sunday mornings when she was a child and take her to the woods. Purposefully, she would miss going to church with my grandmother. My grandfather would sit with her among the trees to watch the squirrels, and he would tell her that she was closer to God there, than in any church. For many years the idea of God living in the woods rather than heaven felt like a daring belief that I could take into my world of the mists between black and white. In my mind's eye, God became a mischievous aging farmer with bib overalls and gray long johns, who wandered the woods with animals and children, and simply tried his best to be a good man.

As a child, I didn't have a word for a feminine face of God, but I had storybooks with Fairy Godmothers and I could see my grandma in that light. As I grew, as often happens when women seek a spiritual connection outside orthodox religion, I embraced the ancient Goddess. And yet, in so doing, I created my own black and white dogma, becoming certain that *She* came first and that restoring Her to Divine standing would solve many challenges of human existence. But there were still pieces that didn't fit. As I grew in my personal belief that Divinity lived within each human being, not just my grandfather, but also the men who had been less than holy to me, I had to look at the women in the same way. Where was my human Goddess? Certainly my grandmother was a wise Crone, who like a Fairy Godmother could do some magical things, but my experience of the Mother brought an awareness of the dark Goddess. Thus my quest for balance and WHOLEness was birthed.

Black and white transformed
Into dark and light
With
Sunrises and sunsets.
The darkest and coldest moments
Of starlit sky
Just before dawn,
And
The first spark of starlight
Just after dusk.

The mists of safety and understanding became the boundless flow through all. And the epiphany was:

As we reclaim the fullness of the Goddess,
We must restore to sacred
Those aspects of God
That have been lost.

Reduced to Abundance

Restoration of the Sacred Masculine is a deeper challenge for many than reclaiming the Sacred Feminine.

Like Jesus, I was raised by a stepdad - actually a step "daddy." He was one of the really good guys on this planet, marrying my mother and taking on a family of three daughters in an era when divorce was not discussed and families as mixed as ours were kept secret. My sisters and I, being three daughters born of the same mother but all different fathers - different "dads" with yet a fourth man, a daddy who raised us as if we were his own. He became my second model for God. I always thought Daddy could teach that Heavenly God the Father a thing or two about how to take care of little girls, and so even to this day I refer to him as my daddy in conscious recognition of a phrase once read: "Anyone can be a father, but it takes someone special to be a daddy." God the Heavenly Father was just like my birth father, completely absent for over thirty-five years of my life. Daddy was a Sacred Masculine expressing as a true Guardian.

Daddy passed away on Father's Day weekend in 2001. I remember my younger sister by his bedside. He lay unconscious in his final hours. "Please don't die on Father's Day" she pleaded. He just adored her and granted her wish by leaving on Saturday night at 11:15 p.m - 45 minutes *before* Father's Day. There was an irony in the experience that reminding me that *nothing* is coincidental, that there is a Divine Purpose, and that Divinity lives in all things. And yet, in those moments and days following his passing, I felt farther away from God than I had ever been. Daddy made God the Father, the Sacred Guardian, *alive* for me.

Yet, like Jesus I had another father. And, while Jesus' "real" father was God, mine had been described to me for my entire life as the Devil himself! On another Father's Day weekend five years prior to Daddy's passing, I began a dance with the Devil when after thirty-five years I found my birth father.

It was 9:00 in the morning on June 19, 1996. On that morning I pulled out a list that had been compiled at my request by U.S. Search. It contained the contact information for every D. Ballentine in the country. I had received it more than 6 months prior, just the latest step in a 20 year on and off search for this man who co-created me. I had not seen or heard from him since Mother moved my older sister and me to Indiana when I was 3 ½ years old. I contacted U.S.Search as part of a therapy process when my counselor pushed me to the limit by saying it was time to "deal with my father shit." Shit indeed!

> The blackest of fertile soil
> From which
> The most beautiful and fragrant lotus is birthed!

When I received the list I decided I wasn't ready to deal with the 3 ½ typed pages, so I filed it in my "DAD" box on a shelf in my closet. Also in the box were pictures, a copy of his and my mom's divorce decree I had obtained from the courts in 1995, and a hand written birth certificate from the hospital where I was born in Prescott, Arizona. Because I was legally adopted by my stepfather, the handwritten certificate was the only document I've ever had with the full collection of his name, my mother's name, and my original name: Patricia Kay Ballentine.

==On that morning in 1996, I was experiencing a rapid succession of nearly heart-stopping synchronicities.== I pulled out the U.S. Search list with an inner knowing that I was being guided and completely supported in what was about to unfold. I picked up the list and made one phone call…one random phone call:

> Pick a name…
> What God or Demon will be revealed today?
> Will he be God the Father
> Holy and Just,
> Out of my life because he's been
> Residing on some great throne
> Someplace in another "state"?

Or will he be the human embodiment of everything evil, like the image I had been give of him for all of those years? Certainly nothing Godlike there! So why was I flirting with, even seeking out a Demon?

> Dance With Darkness
> Daughter of Light.
> Look to the source…
> The center of chaos
> Where all is birthed.
> The womb you emerged from,
> Once expelling you
> Held no connection
> To your inner light…
> Yet from that darkness you were birthed
> With a purpose…
> To Dance With Darkness
> Seeking the balance
> From Him and Her.
> So…
> Was the darkness
> His or Hers?
> *The Darkness is Mine!*

I dialed the telephone number from the list - the one random number. A woman answered the phone, and I said:

"Hello, is David Ballentine there?"

"My son's name is David, why are you calling?"

"My name is Patty and I'm looking for my birth father. He lived in Arizona in the 1950's and he would be in his mid 60's now."

"Yes, my son's name is David and he used to live in Arizona."

I instantly forgot that "guided and connected" piece and dashed right into doubt and fear!

Great…there were two of them and this MUST be the other one because I remember my grandma and she was old THEN! Surely she is long gone by now!

She continued, "He's here. Just a moment and I'll go get him."

My mind was racing. What the hell are you doing? What are you going to say? This can't be right. There must be some weird coincidence.

She returned to the phone and said, "He's getting up. He'll be here in a moment. Where do you live?"

"I live in Phoenix." Then I asked, "What is your name?"

"My name's Cosette."

Oh my God — she's still alive. That means, this is not "the other" but "the one." *Say* something!

"I remember when I was 3 ½ years old my grandma Cosette took a brown paper bag and she cut it so it would lay flat on the ground. She had me lie down on it and she took a crayon and drew an outline around me so that the next time she saw me she could tell how much I had grown."

"Sweetheart, here is my son."

At that moment I lost memory of any more words or sensation of time and space. It felt like she was somehow offering him up to me. It felt as if she were as much the key that I had been searching for as he was. And at the end of the conversation he said, "Well my, oh my. This is quite a gift. My birthday is tomorrow."

God or Demon? That was yet to be revealed, but to be certain contact had been made in the physical realm. It was supported by something mysterious, and yet untapped, from a Higher Source. Even more significant I realized in a heartbeat that I arrived at the time and place where I completely understood that I had taken an action that would change my life forever. I was comfortable accepting responsibility for the outcome. I had twenty years of therapy to deal with being an incest survivor, multiple marriages, co-dependency, and the list could go on, and on, and on. That "in therapy" path all came to an end in the weeks following. I embraced the freedom and responsibility that flowed when I dance with the fullness of Dark and Light.

When all you have thought
About wisdom
Has been reduced
To knowing in your bones what is real for you.

Brow Charka (Third Eye): Spiritual Perspective

Death and Dirty Laundry

The term Domestic Goddess has never been one strongly associated with me. As a child I was simply messy, causing my mother lots of frustration. I drew that forward into adulthood. Fortunately, at some point I understood the importance of picking up after myself. I began taking care of things like laundry before it got to the point of being an overwhelming pile in the corner.

One evening I found myself reflecting on that messy aspect of my life as I was catching up on the laundry. My ironing board was a portable version that fit on my kitchen table. I had just inherited it from my mom who passed away the week before.

I hadn't done any ironing for quite some time and there was a pile to get through. There was a flash of awareness as I observed my laundry as a rather interesting process. Have you ever experienced the stuck laundry cycle? It's where the clothes in the dryer don't make it out before they wrinkle. Then they go back in the washer for a rewet, and during those other times when clothes stay in too long and they are close to being mildewed, they too get washed again. The cycle goes round, and round, and round with no new dirty clothes introduced for quite some time. The net result is that I'd been doing the same load of laundry during the time frame of my mom's illness; I was still looking at the original ironing pile.

That evening I realized my laundry was a pretty good metaphor for some people's life experiences. In looking at the laundry I GOT that it was not an example of my own any more. It was a great mirror that I happily and thankfully said, "Whew - I made it out of the dirty laundry cycle of life!"

During my mom's last couple of months of life, and in the end, her death was a very conscious experience for me. In a sense it was the ultimate opportunity to see if I really walked my talk, believed what I *thought* I believed, and could show up for her in that transition in the way I hoped I could.

One of the things I experienced is the awareness that:
In that moment,
When you are waiting for someone you love
To stay in the pause
Between
The in-breath
And
The out-breath....
When you are waiting for
Their last heartbeat....
Quite often
Your own breath stops
Rather than theirs,
And you feel like
Your heart
Will never beat again.

That is the moment or even the split second when you get a flash of knowing if *you* are authentically alive, or not.

That moment in time as I experienced, was one of the most amazing gifts she ever gave me. Her last breaths took me to the edge of my spiritual practice and inner knowing and then released me to move beyond my self-created limitations. As she now flies free of her body, I fly free as well.

So, what does this have to do with dirty laundry? I realized that a large chunk of my physical and emotional dirty laundry regarding my relationship with my mom had been cleaned up.

Over a number of years I worked through a process of looking at each of the pieces and dealing with them one at a time. Eventually, I could take a group - let's say I color sorted the "stuff" that was interconnected, and processed larger piles more quickly. My mom's death allowed me to look at what had once been mountains of dirty laundry between us and see only a soiled hanky here or there.

Sometimes we are so stuck in that dirty laundry cycle that we never get to the point of making progress on any new dirty clothes. The old patterns and related triggers are so powerful that we allow them to drive us round, and round, and round. Then, depending on our beliefs, we either take them to the grave, or maybe we get to come back in another life and pick up where we left off.

Because I do believe we come around again, I choose to work on cleaning up my life. While I don't believe in going to hell for my sins, coming back in another life and still having my dirty laundry to deal with, isn't really a better option.

Sitting in my cottage with all of that laundry; remnants of Mom's life and passing scattered round my living room floor, and wilting flowers from her memorial service on my kitchen counter, I felt clean in my relationship with her.

I believe that what was significant in the relationship between Mom and me in the last few years of her life, and especially in the last few months, was that she felt like I understood her. What I actually understood and expressed was *my* true self. In being able to do that, it created a safe space for her to work through and let go of some secrets and fears of being judged in this life and after. I understood how it felt to carry the same emotions that she had locked into her own life. That understanding empowered me to guide her through some old wounds, that when revealed enabled *her* to understand herself better, and release some of her own self-judgment. I held the space for her to return to the memories of her walks with her father and embrace a God who lived in the forest, rather than one she was afraid would judge her life.

Mom and I sorted her laundry to see what pile she would choose to tackle at the end of her life. She had some doozies, and there was an obvious place to start. We didn't get it all cleaned up before she died - you never do. But if she comes back around again she'll have less dirty laundry to bring in with her.

As I continued to look around the cottage that evening I had to laugh out loud, because in comparison to my sisters I'm still the messy daughter when it comes to domestic housekeeping, but I'm really comfortable with it. I have learned to set my priorities. There was no energetic charge or reaction when I thought about someone seeing an unorganized living room, the ironing board on my kitchen table and a pile of wrinkled shirts waiting to be pressed. My laundry got behind because I chose to spend every moment I could in the last two months with my mom. That choice blest me with the presence of numerous friends, co-workers and loved ones who saw where I was and completely honored and supported it. They pitched in where they could and I said yes when they asked if I needed what they offered. ==I realized it's a gift to allow someone to truly help you.== There is also no reason to say yes when someone is offering you something you do not need or want. It's not honest and it often comes from a place of assuming we know what they will think or feel if we say no. I choose to allow others to be responsible for their own feelings. It's spiritually and emotionally cleaner for me.

I've made it a practice at the end of every day to look over my day in an absolutely truthful and gratitude-filled reflection. I mean really, who am I going to hide from in the moments before I fall asleep? I believe "God" had been inside of me all day long and I'm pretty sure She knew when I wasn't being authentic. I'm also sure She experienced my struggles with love and acceptance and sent an energetic boost to help me learn and grow as the next day dawned. I own my mistakes and my triumphs and I sleep very well each night.

> I Choose…
> To choose
> To grow
> To be humble
> To be proud
> I choose to BE awake.

I may never forget the image of Mom's last breath. It wasn't pretty and it wasn't peaceful. But as her spirit left her body there was beauty and peace for both of us.

> And we each emerged
> Into the next phase
> Of a still unfolding journey
> With new awareness…

Reduced to Abundance

I spent nearly three hours writing this tonight. I didn't get any more ironing done. The washer is silent, as is the dryer. I can't tell you right now if there are clothes in either one but I know I'm clean.

> I know nothing inside of me is
> Going round, and round, and round
> That like my mom
> My essence is not my body
> Or my dirty or clean laundry.
> My essence is intact and free.

My mom's spirit left her body last week never to return in this lifetime. I celebrate the relationship between the two of us that evolved and in the end felt authentic and remarkably clean. I miss her blue eyes and the hours we spent together in the last year laughing, sewing, "gettin' into mischief," learning about each other in a new way. But I'm here and whole and feeling grateful for the conscious experience of her passing as strange as that may sound.

> She never thought I was a very good housekeeper
> But
> I'm pretty sure she's proud of how I handle my laundry.
> It was a gift to HER…
> As well.

When all you have been told
About when to speak and what to say
Has been reduced
To your own authentic words.

Throat Chakra: Speaking our truth

I Can't Tell You That I'm Sorry

In sorting through some of my mom's papers after she passed away, my sister came across a card that I had given to Mom and Daddy on one of their wedding anniversaries. I remember seeing it tucked in the family Bible at one time. Although it wasn't dated, I could tell it was sent when I was in my very early 20's and already married and divorced for the first of four times. My handwritten words were telling them how sorry I was for being such a challenging and disappointing daughter. I vowed to change and make them proud of me. I pledged it would be so! As I was looking at this card my first thought was: of the dozens of cards I must have given them over the years why was this the only one kept? I was struck by the irony of it being preserved in the Bible, anchoring my vow with God's word!

I Thought I Knew…
Who God was and
Where He lived,
What
Defined success
And being a Good Person.
I thought I knew
Because I listened to
What I had been told,
And believed
How I had been raised.
And then…
I Remembered…
What I knew before the first
Human word was
Spoken into my ear
Or the first human experience unfolded!

> I just *didn't* remember…
> How to
> Gracefully
> Painlessly
> Instantaneously
> UnDo…
> Or release
> All that I had already done.

Rereading the words on the card, I could see my 20 year old self literally at the threshold of the conscious journey, of remembering who I "came to *be*" in this lifetime. I could touch the memory of thinking I was responsible, not only for my personal pain but a great deal of what I then perceived as my parents' pain. I was telling them I was sorry for being a "bad" daughter. However, reaching back through time I was aware, even then, that I was *really* saying, "I'm sorry for being confused, and hurt and unhappy." Also I was saying, "I'm sorry for the discomfort of what is yet to come."

I don't know if it was because of the *"birth order"* thing and being the middle daughter, but I do know it was part of my personal life journey to *stir* the family pot! For whatever reason I have the ability to remember obscure details and comments and put pieces of life puzzles together. That also means I have the ability to see where the pieces don't fit, to understand the significance of embracing the whole picture. I am not afraid to ask tough questions and hear tougher answers. I have also honed a profoundly significant acquired skill: I rarely hold a grudge.

One of the lessons I've learned over the years is that although what I ultimately search for is "truth," truth is an elusive thing. It's all about perception. And on top of the perception is often an overlay, or filter of a personal wish that an experience had actually "been" different. Since thought is a very powerful thing, I have the ability *to make my wishes true.*

I also have the ability to remember an experience from only my own perspective. In so doing, I am the Creator of my personal pleasure or pain. I have blocked out pieces that were too painful to think about, or focused on them to the point that they created an underlying current of unhappiness that flowed through my life for years. I have felt judged for exploring family memories that were painful with those who just want everything to be "nice."

Years ago, my younger sister gave me a fabulous vision of how this "looks." She was advising me to get a pair of very dark sunglasses, so that no one could see if I was looking at them, and no one could see if I was crying. I realized that we three sisters all wore very different lenses that served, not only as our filters and influenced our perception, but also served as our means of protection. My younger sister's dark lenses had created an air of mystery around her as she guarded her heart and her story. My older sister wore the rose colored lenses through which she desired to see everything as loving and without conflict. Mine were magnifiers. Because of our different lenses we saw life at home and each other in very different ways. Those differences, carried into adulthood, created underlying currents of separation and misunderstanding that were not healed until we were each able to see and then hear the other's point of view. I had to remove my magnifiers to enable me to look at my older sister in a gentler way, and the older sister had to take off her rose-colored glasses and realize the pain that had been hidden by the dark lenses of her youngest sister. We didn't have to embrace that point of view, but certainly needed to acknowledge its existence as "true" to the other sister. When we were able to remove the lenses of protection and separation we were able to see the common territory of our family and experience a clearer understanding of how we were connected. Attachment to the good or bad of an experience faded into the mists, and judgment was sometimes reduced, if not released.

In many ways, I didn't know the fullness of who my parents were. I only knew my experience and perception of them. It wasn't until I was a grown adult, using my magnifier lenses and gathering pieces of the family puzzle by poking into uncomfortable places, that I realized my mother and I had experienced the same type of abuse as children. I realized that the words she spoke to me were the very words *her* mother had spoken to her. They were words that made a child responsible for her own pain, and transformed a violation into shame. It was one of those very brief conversations where she was responding to a question I had asked about my childhood abuse. Her statement was intended to offer rationalization that it really wasn't so bad because it had happened to her. The words came tumbling out through her lips, and I could almost see her trying to catch each one with her hands and stuff them back into the darkness of her own pain.

That was the moment I realized *I couldn't tell her I was sorry* for being such a challenge, because I no longer needed to hear *her* say she was sorry she wasn't a better mother. I didn't need to hear her say she was sorry she didn't protect me. I realized that there is always a story behind the story. The energetic charge I got from holding onto my personal shame and pain was significantly transformed in a heartbeat. I couldn't blame her anymore for what I had chosen to hold.

The Mother in me
Wanted to embrace the wounded child
In Her.
And
The child in me
Received
With compassionate understanding
The love
Of a wounded Mother.

There is one last piece in this bit of life tapestry. I realized that in my resistance to engage my mom when the conversations revealed a corner of a wound or a grudge that she had carried for over 70 years, I was seeing her as too old to change, release, or to grow. I was using her for information to support my personal transformation, but I wasn't sharing with her the fullness of the experience. I was taking and not giving the gift of healing.

Ironically, my mom was legally blind in one eye and had severely compromised vision in the other. She chose to not see much of what had evolved in our family, and yet, when reduced to the simplest understanding, like her daughters, her lenses were her tools and her protection.

Reduced to Abundance

Mom created complex stories that became true for her. They were held so strongly that she lost understanding of how anyone else's eyes could see more than she did. Just after Christmas one year she and I were sitting at her kitchen table and I mentioned my birth father. Her immediate response was the retelling of a story that I had heard a hundred times in my lifetime. It was a story of her abandonment and pain. When she had finished, I calmly said to her, "Mom, I don't need to hear that story any more. In all these years I have not heard one positive thing about the man who birthed me with you. He, after all of these years, is not the man you remember." And then I asked, "Do you want to be seen today, as the memory he has of the person you were 50 years ago?"

She fell silent for a moment and then said "No."

I gently responded, "Then you don't get to judge him today."

She proved invalid my perception that she was too old to see things differently, or too set in her ways to engage in healing through challenge, and a corner of her wound was released.

So, Today…

I can't tell you that I'm sorry for being the problem child, or for coming in as "the change agent" of the family. I saw life through magnifiers and refused to be silenced by the family secrets. I am not sorry for being willing to risk the image of being an *ordinary family member* in order to live an extraordinarily honest and authentic life.

Today, as I draw that past experience into present consciousness, the message I would write in a card to my parents would be different:

Dear Mom and Daddy,

I can't tell you that I'm sorry, and I understand why you never said it to me.

Instead, I'm thankful for the moments in which we removed the lenses of separation and understood how differently love looked to each of us.

I continued to be a challenge until the very end of both your lives didn't I?

I'm so glad we know now that was part of my job in our family. I was called to push the envelope, probe the pain, bring clarity to the confusion, and draw forth the unthinkable from the darkness of fear into the light of love.

Let's all pick something easier to remember, when we come 'round the next time!

I love you,
Patty

When all you have shared
As love
Has been reduced
To integrated thoughts and feelings flowing from the heart.

Heart Chakra: Love & Trust

Blessings of The Stranger

Being told from a young age "not to talk to strangers" seemed ironic for me. Thinking of my childhood experiences, I often felt physically safer facing a stranger on the street than a family member. I would hear anger in my mother's voice as I, in my innocence, shared a conversation I'd had with someone new. Her underlying fear came from her desire to keep family secrets, rather than wanting to keep me safe. As an eight or nine year old I didn't understand yet what the secrets actually were. I was often just spontaneously sharing "my family does this" in response to a comment from another child. Over time I began to withhold words, curiosity and laughter. Fear of my mother's reactions transformed my interactions to reserved and often untrue conversation. I would make things up rather than risk her anger with an honest response. And yet the childhood lies, when discovered, were shameful as well. This was a profound experience of innocence lost at an early age.

As years passed, that spontaneous child, Patty was buried under layers of thoughts and feelings that were not of my creation, but became what I expressed through my actions. In its most detrimental manifestation, "Don't talk to a stranger" became my reaction when my inner child spoke up from within my BEing. She patiently but persistently challenged me to look within and bring her back to the surface of my life. Thankfully, she was a strong-willed child. Over the years she fought her way from the inner stillness, causing chaos and lots of tears as she demonstrated her fierce quest for expression!

And as *she* re-emerged
I became a different person
Who was not as "familiar" to family members.
Not as comfortable to be around.
As I became me
To my family

Patricia Ballentine

I *became*
The Stranger.

In 1996, when I found my birth father and my grandmother, my first thought was to delve through all of the unanswered questions regarding the last thirty-five years. I wanted to understand what had happened and fill in all of the gaps. I was searching for that illusive "truth" that was so important to me. On our first visit I showed up as the well-prepared interrogator inquiring about the stories my mother had told that formed the image I carried of my father. I wanted everything she had said to be absolutely true and at the same time I wanted it all to be a complete lie. If he were a horrible man, I would have missed nothing by his absence in my life all of those years and she would have been righteous in her fierce determination that we never see or hear from him. On the other hand, if he was not the man she described, how could I survive what I perceived as the impending grief of all of those years without him in my life to love me and to be loved by me?

It was a peaceful afternoon as I sat in Dad and Grandma Cosette's small living room. I faced these two people who were strangers to me, yet part of my very essence. Dad was a weather worn man. The years of working outdoors showed in the lines upon his face. He had a piercing look, yet he rested his hands on the arm of his chair in a way that appeared relaxed and comfortable with the life altering conversation that unfolded. He was tall and lean, and as I looked at him I wondered at what age I lost the ability to recall what he looked like. Surely there had been memories of sitting on his lap or holding his hand. When did I lose the sound of his voice? My memories had been influenced by years of others' projections and I had surrendered to them what had been mine in the beginning.

I did remember Cosette. I realized that I had been able to hold onto my childhood memory of her because I never shared it with anyone as I was growing up. This prevented the opportunity for outside input and perceptions to change it in any way. Like a secret gem, I savored the memory of the color of her hair, the way she dressed; the very words she spoke to this little child at the age of 3 ½.

As conversation began to flow that day, I was struck by the grace with which they each answered my probing questions and also by the number of things we had in common.

Cosette was a fine pastel artist who, in her 80's, had stopped creating beautiful images. I was an emerging artist-at-heart and felt an immediate connection. I was the answer to her unspoken question, "Who shall inherit the gift of my lifetime of collected art supplies?"

Dad and I shared a love of the exploration of ancient civilizations and archeology, certain types of music, and writers. We all had wounds and triumphs. Through the hours of that first meeting we embraced the freedom to move through and release the thoughts and feelings built up over the years that created images of all that we each *were not*. I was not a lost 3 ½ year old child, Cosette was not a radiant redhead any more, and my father was not the Devil incarnate. We were strangers whose only real link was genetic, yet what a sacred experience to be able to embrace a stranger through a cleared heart void of projected judgment or fear. In the months and years to follow, my heart became filled with thoughts and feelings about them that I completely owned - dark and light - mine.

<blockquote>
Behind the curious eyes of my father
Whose gaze
Is new and inviting
Resides a Stranger
Who welcomes
Me home.
</blockquote>

At that time, however, the opportunity to release and heal was not yet my mother's choice. Within the week after that first meeting, she and I sat in a local coffee shop on a Sunday afternoon where as casually, but clearly as possible, I explained that I had found Dad and Cosette. There was an immediate flash of fire from her eyes that I recognized as anger, yet I saw through to the fear behind the flash. Her strikes about why I needed to do such a terrible thing were intermixed with yet another repeat of the stories I had heard over and over about Dad. Included was the one piece she had often spoken. "I can still see Cosette's coal black eyes."

Such a simple statement, but when heard this last time brought another heartbeat of transformation. I then knew, my grandmother's eyes were a pale blue that sparkled from an ivory face of a tiny, white-haired, Irish woman. I understood as I looked into my mother's face that I couldn't really say she had lied, although she had certainly created her own reality. A lifetime of complex stories, created in the beginning for reasons that remained hers alone to share, had been told with such need and conviction for so many years. It all became true for her. She really believed that I had seen Cosette's eyes as "black as coal." I saw no purpose in challenging her memory in that moment. Her healing would come in her own time and in the way of her choosing nearly 10 years later.

In the last few weeks of Mom's life, she and I spent hours reviewing her joys and her pain. We worked to honor the gifts of her lifetime, and release the wounds she could. One afternoon as I sat on the edge of her hospital bed we chose a page in the back of a journal she had started years before. I drew a circle within which she placed her greatest joys and blessings. On the outside of the circle were the names of people associated with unfinished business and wounds, the oldest and most violating represented by a symbol because she could not bear to write the name. One by one, we processed those pieces. My dad's name was included with those on that outside space, and in her last few days she acknowledged the need to let go of the wound. However, she was not able to completely move the energy to a place of release. And the face behind the symbol – that was never approached.

In the last hours of her life, as she lay unconscious, my work to assist her transition continued and at the suggestion of a dear friend, we called my dad on the phone from her bedside and invited him to try and remember a time 50 years ago when he loved her. We invited him to hold that memory in his consciousness and his heart, sending her loving thoughts and energy to support her transition. Dad hadn't seen her now for forty-five years and there had been bitter memories on both sides. He acknowledged that yes, he could do that. He still remembered when they were in love with each other. He chose to move past any of his own bitterness to a place of love and held that thought to assist her journey. From hundreds of miles and lifetimes away my father, now a stranger to her, reached out from the distance, with a loving thought that had the power to touch the last hours of her life. I could feel it and I knew that even though she was not conscious, it assisted her spirit in releasing from her body. For a moment, though miles apart, my mother, my father, and I were closer than we had ever been.

Memories,
Do they damn us
Or
Are they our salvation
Cast in stone or as shifting as the sands?
The only certainty
Is that everything…
Even stone
Changes.

*When all you have manifested
From a position of power
Has been reduced
To a powerful, personal presence.*

Solar Plexus Chakra: Self-Respect & Integrity

Wild Child!

I was an olive thief as a child. When no one was home I snuck into the kitchen pantry, opened the new jar of olives, and over the course of a week, one at a time, ate half of the jar. I never had a clue it would be noticed they were gone or that it would be so easy to figure out who ate them. I was the only daughter who liked olives, the only real suspect in this olive caper. One might wonder how I could be so naive as to think I would get away with such an obvious crime? Certainly over the years that question was part of a legendary family tale shared with lots of laughter at my ignorance. How indeed, can anyone be unconscious, unaware, uninformed, inexperienced? Inquiring minds want to know. Yet through the inquisition the subject (or thief in this case) is often reduced to embarrassment or shame until we clean up the wound. We then finally respond at what becomes the final telling of the tale with something like, "Why do *you* need to keep telling that story, because I am done with it."

As a child, besides loving olives, I loved art. Into my teens and early 20's I aspired to be an artist and it was one of the few subjects in high school I enjoyed. I can't say I excelled in it because classes didn't feel "inspiring" to me. However, I was able to create art that was seen as pretty and brought positive attention to me. Well, usually positive, because there were experiences like that one class when we were learning about calligraphy. My project resulted in a lovely poster with the words:

> *Two are better than one*
> *If two lie together they have heat*
> *But, how can one be warm alone?*

Inappropriate? What do ya mean? It is right out of the Bible! Oh, and there was the creative writing class where I composed a poem about being black, except there weren't any black students in our school, and that was the point.

> Just yesterday we walked side by side
> On the soft sandy beach
> Just watching the tide.
> We talked about life
> And how it would be
> If all of the world felt like you
> Like me.

It was two pages long and ended with:

> Did you leave me my friend
> Just because I am black?

It was the early 70's in a small town in the Midwest. I was a girl who already wasn't fitting in her family of origin. I was pushing the envelope of self-discovery and on top of that, I wanted to study drafting along with my art. It generated one more *no* from a school advisor who said drafting was for boys.

Hey teachers, parents and advisors: I'm not feeling very empowered here! I'm still a kid and don't even know what "empowered" is, but I'm *reacting* and getting resentful!

Typical teen? I hope not. There was an underlying core wound that was amplifying how I expressed myself. Yet, because I wasn't one of the more volatile students, (I was very sneaky and pretty darned bright) I was flying under the radar of the school counselors. I was drinking at school, sexually active and in a hurry to do whatever I needed to get away from home as soon as I could. And yet I *never* got caught, got pregnant, or had an accident.

After graduating from high school I enrolled in a commercial art program at a technical school in the neighboring "big city" of Fort Wayne, Indiana. Within the first month of class, the instructor held up one of my assignments, along with a couple of other students' work and announced to the class "This Stinks!" I walked out of the class, put away my art supplies and did not paint anything but walls again for nearly 25 years.

Within a matter of months I was hired by the General Electric Company to be part of their Toolmaker Machinist Apprenticeship program assisted by an affirmative action plan requiring them to look for women and minorities. And hey, guess what? I was not only learning to be a drafter, I was working with people of color! (I couldn't make up the amazing weaving of these pieces!) Patty became Pat, because in the early 70's women in the world of machine design and engineering were rare, even with affirmative action. The name Patty in the title block of my drawings got more feedback from the people who were ending up with them in their hands, than the mechanical components I was designing. "Pat" could be Patrick so it was who I became. As long as there wasn't a phone conversation, I was still flying under someone's radar.

Very early in what became a 40-year career in engineering and industrial design, I had the opportunity to experience one of the most extraordinary teachers of my life. His name was Jerry and he was my mentor at a small tool and die shop. The flash of transformation came when I realized what a gift "This Stinks" was for without it, I would have missed the friendship and guidance of one of the most powerful men I've ever known.

Jerry was a survivor of polio and the disease's effect on his body was extremely apparent. With the torso of an adult man, and the legs of a very young boy, his spine had more than 90 degrees of curve. But, to me the most mesmerizing features of his physical appearance were his smile and his beautiful hands. I have no idea why I hold such a strong memory of his hands, other than as my mentor, I would watch how he held his mechanical pencils and pound out formulas on his calculator. He taught me to use the dial calipers, micrometers and other measurement tools of the trade. When he and his wife were planning to have their second child, he was delighted. I remember that he took a penny and held it between his thumb and middle finger and tap, tap, tap, tapped it on the desk with a flash of his smile showing me how frequently they were practicing to get it right!

Jerry was a patient teacher who encouraged me through a three-year work/study experience. Working side by side, I watched the steps he would take to design a die and I learned the discipline and organization of the craft. And more significantly, I learned some enduring lessons of how to be an adult. During this time I began taking the first steps toward self-responsibility.

In my view, there was nothing that Jerry couldn't do. Married, the father of two, deeply in love with his family, he had a successful career. He even designed and built his own house. He didn't see his body or the life experiences that had been part of his childhood as negative or things to overcome. Jerry expressed an outrageous sense of humor, phenomenal tenderness, and extremely high intelligence. His imprint was placed upon my soul even though he left the planet at age 38. Post-polio syndrome had caused the "healthy" structure of his body to over compensate for the balance and the result was premature deterioration. One of his last conversations with me was a phone call from his hospital where they had surgically straightened his spine, added steel rods and screwed a stainless "crown" to his skull to prevent his chest cavity from crushing his lungs. "Hey, I grew" he said, "I always wanted to be taller!"

Jerry was a giant to me. He raised me up, making me feel smart and creative. He inspired me to make the very best of my career. And yet, it was a deeper piece. Someone outside of my *self* helped me realize that being smart was not the same thing as owning my own intelligence, creativity, and BEing. He created and held a space for me to adjust my perspective. It was like lifting a corner on a lovely box that contains the magnificent me inside. It took me years to see that his greatest gift was the way he owned his life. It is what made him such a powerful presence and model for me.

My career grew and evolved over the years, shifting into self-employment, co-founding a company with the father of my sons. Another shift took me to running a one-woman, home-based business, doing reverse engineering for heavy equipment manufacturers across the country. When my sons were still living at home, blueprints were frequently strewn across my kitchen table. One son was my hardware and software guru and the other was my AutoCAD drawing checker.

Yet…it was a piece of artwork that brought forth the truly powerful presence within my BEing.

Machines drawn from my mind

Supporting my family
And filling a place in
My life…
DOing it well.
Images emerging from my soul
Connecting to my passion
And revealing a place in
My life…
BEing expressed!

Early in 1996 that urge to find my birth father was flaring after my counselor had urged me to deal with that "Father Shit." I had received the list from U.S. Search and had packed it away in the Dad Box. I had also just experienced my first women's ceremonial circle.

It was a Full Moon and we drummed, danced, told stories and watched the magnificence of the moon rising above the horizon. At the end of the evening, I experienced an overwhelming urge to capture something about the evening in a sketch, and the only piece of paper that I had was a 24 x 36 piece of drafting vellum. With kitchen plates as templates, the sketch evolved into nine, salad-plate-size moons with images in each. In the lower corner there were three women dancing. One with a drum, one with a flute, and one with amazing feather wings. Their movement and notes and percussive energies moved from their bodies and instruments and surrounded the moons. When the sketch was complete, I dug into a box of things from an ancient past and found a Prang watercolor set from high school, a sharpie marker, ballpoint pens, colored pencils and table salt. The sketch developed depth, texture and color.

When the image was done, I took the artwork to my therapist and we processed the power of the BEing behind the art. It was the day after my therapy session that I pulled out the list, made the call, and found my birth father. I stepped into the powerful BEing that my dear friend and mentor Jerry had modeled to me so very many years before.

*When all you have desired
From a relationship with others
Has been reduced
To the dance of the Inner Lover.*

Sacral Chakra: Creativity and Sexuality

My Story behind My Story

The question is, how long does a moment last? Really?

When I was about three years old, I decided I was going to take a big collie for a walk. As I grabbed the end of her leash, she saw something down the street worth dashing toward. She lunged, dragging me along. I bloodied my knees and wet my pants, but was gathered up in concerned arms, loved and got band-aids and fresh clothes, hugs and kisses. The dog was not around our family much longer. And it seemed everyone lived happily ever after - for the moment. And in life, really, that's all there is… the moment.

In another moment, two years later, I was alone with a family member who put himself inside my body. There was no one there to see what happened. No one there to immediately gather me up in their arms and wrap me in love and hugs and kisses. For me, that moment lasted days because it began with words of what a "good" thing it was going to be, and yet ended in, "Tell no one." So I didn't tell anyone immediately. And when I did, as I stood in the dining room of my aunt and uncle's home looking out the picture window toward the mobile home of this family member who did the "good," yet unspeakable deed:

> I was asked by my mother, "Did you bleed?"
> *Oh, if only I had.*
> Perhaps *then* I would have been picked up
> In her arms and wrapped in love and hugs and kisses
> And
> Gotten band-aids and fresh clothes.
> Instead
> I was told
> "Don't go back in there."
> But, I did,
> And this time I didn't tell.

Because I was
A child and I was ashamed
Because I did something
My mother
Told me
Not to do.
And for a moment…
I was a shameful, responsible person.
And that moment…lasted decades.

In time my physical experience was compounded by the mental awareness that the family member was not shipped away like the dog. I not only embraced the concept that I was responsible for the experience, but also with time I lost contact with the child within me who knew what the core wound actually was. Thus, as an adult I spent years trying to figure out how to heal something that was in fact not wounded. I searched for ways to fix something that was not broken.

In the absolute actual moment that I was attacked, as a five-year-old child I had nothing in my range of experience that said this was a "different" kind of hurt than being slapped by an adult. The physical pain was no more intense than accidents I had already experienced in my young life. The core wound was created by the first words that described this experience as something to be hidden, lied about, and finally something to be *asham*ed of. Shame, not penetration, anchored my belief that nothing pleasurable should be associated with or flow from that part of my body.

As I grew into womanhood, shame was fed by everything: from my mother's discomfort and lack of preparedness at the onset of my menstrual cycle, to the cultural denial of anything holy and awe inspiring about orgasmic sexual union. I had no reference that my body was a sacred portal to life and that it held the potential for deep, intimate pleasure. I was a woman misinformed yet obsessed with sex. My actions were uneducated, unfulfilling, and dangerous.

The men I drew into my life were as wounded as I. Although they were orgasmic, they were no more educated than I about a woman's body *or* their own. The same cultural denial that held out of balance my understanding of pleasure set them in an equally unhealthy role as aggressor or performer. We did not connect as conscious, intimate partners and co-creators.

As I searched for someone who could bring me sexual satisfaction, it seemed I journeyed further from the potential to heal my core wound. I was focused on fixing a body that "didn't function" rather than healing the moment I was shamed and truly lost my innocence.

> Lost? Misplaced.
> My womanhood?
> My childlike innocence
> And sense of
> Self and safety.
> Focusing between my legs
> Rather than
> My core.

As I was shamed, so I shamed others. My lack of satisfaction was projected on those who tried their best to bring me pleasure, deepening their own wounds. Though there was a part of me that secretly believed my body no longer had whatever that "part" was that served as the keyway to ecstasy, I still expected my partners to not only bring the key, but also find that missing portal. My body was infinitely wise, not wounded. Although experiencing ecstasy may have given me profound pleasure it would not have healed my emotional wounds.

It was the birth of my first son that created the first heartbeat of healing my true wound. I looked at the magnificence of every piece of his tiny body and saw him as a complete treasure. Waves of anxiety swept over me however, as I realized the tremendous responsibility of bringing a child into the world. Then I received the flash of clarity. I realized I didn't want my son to be like me. I recognized he was born without shame, and that I already *was* my mother as one who passed along the lineage of shaming others. I began to realize the layers and complexity woven into my life by lack of knowledge and the stage that is set by generations of secrets. In order to save my son from my *self*, I had to find the child that I had been and restore something lost that I couldn't yet even imagine.

There are some wonderful therapists and there are some who are not. In 20 years, I experienced the full range, and in the end, I realized even the best did not hold the key to my healing, but provided tools. I also learned that the secrets were mine and apparently well hidden. Many whom I thought were the best therapists, missed the wound and focused on the sexual attack, which often simply increased my sexual frustration.

My personal portal of pleasure was not about to bring itself to light until the core wound was first named. The birth of my son drove me into therapy. Years later, reading Riane Eisler's book *Sacred Pleasure* crystallized my awareness of shame and introduced me to The Goddess in her many manifestations. Also reaffirmed were aspects of God I had only touched from my childhood, re-visioning who and what HE was. One of the most emotionally challenging books I've ever read, *Sacred Pleasure* not only named my shame but revealed to me the magnitude of the disease. Projected as a fundamental practice, it wove its way back through my family of origin, through the traditional Catholic family I had married into - literally, back through thousands of years. In a heartbeat, I realized that I was not a shameful woman, but an aspect of the gem of Feminine Divinity whose time had come to be restored.

Restoration is a long journey in itself. The flash of awareness does not heal the wound instantaneously, because shame had wrapped itself into my thoughts, feelings, and actions. Just like an alcoholic who becomes "sober," it takes a while for the feet to walk the talk.

And yet, by naming the true wound, an opportunity for another aspect of God as the Sacred Sexual Partner, entered in the form of a "Nice Italian Man." He was older, conscious and skilled at touch and engaging true intimacy. My first experience of orgasm was the result of his encouragement and my ability to finally look at and explore my body with love and acceptance. This Sacred Partner was the first man to show me what reverence for the body looked and felt like. It was through his eyes I heard the first description of my portal to pleasure. It was totally unique like petals of a blossom, no two alike. I was thirty-five years old, opening in the absolutely perfect setting, with the full conscious engaging of this partner and myself.

I can't imagine what thoughts those first flutters of orgasmic awakening would have stirred for me in a different time and place. Would my life have unfolded differently? Absolutely! But it serves no higher purpose to put energy into "what ifs" rather than to stay present in "what is." The depth of the gratitude I experienced for the wisdom and expression of my own body came from a place of maturity, yet brought back to safe consciousness and creative expression the playful child.

She, The Child,
And I, The Mother
Became one again.
And with the embracing of my body Wisdom
We were the Feminine Holy Trinity
The Maiden, The Mother and The Crone.

When all you have felt was safe
And provided shelter
Has been reduced
To essential existence.

Root Chakra: Foundation

The Apple of my Grandma's Eye

If an apple falls from an uphill tree,
Rolling under another apple tree
And
There is no one in the grove to see it move...
Whose apple is it, anyway?

My papa may have been a rolling stone, but my mama was just one tree in a family grove. At any given moment, aunts, sisters, cousins and Grandma were all playing the role of mother. I have one older cousin who, to this day, says she always felt closer to my mother than her own. She seriously pondered the possibility that Mother gave birth to her and then somehow offered the babe to the older sister to raise. And frankly, who knows? Just about anything is possible in my family of origin.

There were times that I liked my cousin's mom best. As a first grader I walked past my aunt's corner grocery and she watched from the window. She motioned me inside to make a selection from the penny candy counter. *Boy*, did that feel like love.

There was also an extended period of time when my mother was hospitalized for a back injury and my grandma filled the mother role. Certainly "nuclear family" is not a term that describes my childhood experience. In fact, it was multi-generational and extended. Like the roots below the surface, the grove of relationships were intertwined and often enmeshed and impeding on the territory of the other family member's boundaries. The real challenge was that my family wasn't conscious of what boundaries were, hence the depth of the enmeshment.

I do not believe my sisters and I, though half-sisters, ever viewed ourselves as anything less than *fully* sisters. Of course there was rivalry, and my personal description of our trinity as young adults was, "My older sister is the smart one, my younger sister is the pretty one, and

I'm the middle kid." In truth, we were all "only" children; the dynamic of our mother's relationship with each of our fathers (or lack thereof) dramatically impacted her relationship with each of us on many levels of consciousness.

I felt like the loathsome child, because my mother loathed my father. Over the years I developed perceptions and projected opinions about each of my sisters based on how I saw their individual relationship with Mom. But I didn't understand that their personal stories were much different than the ones I created about each of them. All three of us experienced the absence of our birth fathers in different ways. The only common word describing how we felt might be incomplete, yet the unfolding of that sense was as diverse as the genes we each received from our fathers.

Typical sibling rivalry was alive and well with its "Mama and Daddy loved *you* best," yet there was something else at play - something deeper, hidden, yet as apparent as the differences in our appearance. And it was that visual reminder that spurred me on to find answers for myself, leading me to the wearing of my magnifier lenses. The obvious, but unspeakable, drove my younger sister behind her dark lenses of protection, and my older sister to the role of wearer of the rose-colored lenses.

By first grade, my daddy (stepdad) had come into the picture, marrying Mother and re-creating our version of a very blended but nuclear family. We moved to the nearest small town where my aunt and uncle owned the corner grocery. Daddy's actions removed us from harm's way of life on the farm, however much had already been cast in the lives of each member of this family. Certainly the community knew more about our family business than my mother was comfortable with. Though we'd moved from the farm, stories of Mom's multiple marriages were known by the town folk. I believe she was ready to try to leave the past behind and start a fresh life, again. Unfortunately, Mom's way of starting over always involved more layers of secrets and we, as children, were drawn deeper into the confusion and darkness that secrets create.

The name Patty K. Ballentine was lost to me in the third grade. It was taken away by a legal adoption that replaced Ballentine, with a name that I could not even spell, upon entering a new school, in a new town.

I was a new child birthed by the shrouding of all I had been up to that point. I can still remember adding the next layer of shame. I was being asked my name and feeling the grief of the child lost, as I fumbled for how to spell the "new" name the teacher was reading on my paper. And I didn't spell it right. The teacher's response launched the laughter and ridicule of the children. It was brutal, "The new girl is stupid. She can't even spell her name!"

I created a neatly boxed package labeled "Patty K. Ballentine", containing my brief eight years of history on this planet. In a sense, I sealed it up, and with time it was placed on a shelf right next to my "Dad Box." This package would wait for a time when I chose to revisit my own early history. When the time was right I would reach back with the support of tools, inspiration, self-love and acceptance to remove the lid, embrace the contents and allow the healing to transform my life.

The child I became, and the woman I grew into, was the daughter of well-intentioned parents. In many ways feeling disconnected from my family was as much a blessing as a curse. Once I left home at 18, I didn't feel obligated to take Mother and Daddy's advice about how to live life. At some level of consciousness I wanted them to be proud, but I had a fierce desire to do things my way. Unfortunately, I did not have a solid foundation that included an understanding of compassion. I rolled over lots of people along my journey. Was that my genetic link to my papa the rolling stone?

Ballentine. I can hear it spoken within my mind and imagination, in the Scottish brogue that, try as I might, cannot roll off my own tongue with ease. Like the memory of my grandma Cosette, I held the name close to my heart. As I began to search for my birth father, and my inner lost child, I explored the roots of this ancient Scottish name. It was the name that led me to the practices of ancient Celts. It brought explanations of the rhythmic flow of the seasons and life, to the myths of a God who walked the forest with the animals not unlike my childhood vision of my Grandfather. If my mother's family was the apple grove of my life, my Scottish ancestry was the very soil I came from. The internal draw I felt to what I was learning re-sparked an aspect from my childhood memory. I saw castles in the clouds, played with flower companions and danced with the energy of my imagination.

Introductions to completely different cultures and religious beliefs created a new backdrop for my personal family story. *What if*:

> An apple fell from an uphill tree
> Rolling under another tree
> Stopping
> Exactly where
> It was
> Supposed to BE?

Inspiration was re-birthed by the re-igniting of that spark of imagination. It quickly expanded and burst into bright expression on that moonlit night in a women's full moon ceremonial circle! It was Patty K. Ballentine, the winged dancer, connecting with salad plate size moons on the artwork that took life on a 24 x 36 piece of drafting vellum. And it was the child Patty K. who found her father after thirty-five years of separation, within days of her awakening.

My younger sister and my grandma Cosette held the final keys to the story of my childhood. After finding my father I pondered for several years whether or not to reclaim my birth name. Through adoption and four marriages I had worn a litany of names. I held onto a false sense of responsibility for my mother's feeling, knowing how she still bristled at the mention of Ballentine. She worked so hard to purge it from me.

During the last months of Grandma Cosette's life, I had made a commitment to study the ancient wheel of the year with a Wiccan High Priestess. I was working on taking responsibility for my life in an even deeper way, releasing fears and a false sense of responsibility for others feelings. There came a time to ritually die to my old self and birth a new me. It was autumn, and Cosette had passed away that summer. I had come to the decision that I was ready to choose to become Patricia K. Ballentine again. Part of me wished I had spoken those words to Cosette while I was still able to peer into her pale blue eyes. I did call my father and shared my decision with him. He was tearful and understood the depth of the choice.

Reduced to Abundance

As I was preparing my clothes that evening, the telephone rang. It was my younger sister. She said, "I heard from Mom that Cosette passed away this summer. I was just wondering, did you ever talk to her and David about me?"

You see, the lenses my younger sister wore were the color of her large, dark brown eyes. Mother said this caramel skinned beauty resembled my grandmother Cosette, with the coal black eyes. She had been told her entire life that my father was her father, and that she looked like Cosette.

I answered, "Yes, we talked about you often. We are all certain that my Dad is not your father. Cosette was a tiny, ivory skinned, blue-eyed woman."

Over the years I had frequently questioned my mother and she held fast to her reality even when I reasoned aggressively and logically that my sister knew nothing about 50% of her medical history and deserved that information. There was a point in time, years earlier, when I told my sister everything I believed I knew, but without knowing Cosette - it was simply my story verses Mom's.

When I found Cosette, my mother realized I knew the truth. She could not bear to see it revealed. So she did her best to drive even deeper wedges between my sisters and me.

On this night the adult woman within me was preparing to reclaim the child, and the name I came into this life with. My younger sister, not knowing what I was doing, said to me, "If I just knew what my father's name was, I would use it." And then she asked if I would talk to Mom again. Over the years she tried and tried. All our mother would ever say was that she had Cosette's eyes.

> Sweet Sister -
> I held your hand
> And took you
> Through the veils with me
> On that night.

Within a week after my rebirth, I went to our mother with clarity and a new voice requesting she reveal the truth. As Mom began with the same description of Cosette, I paused and then responded, "Mama, her eyes were as blue as mine and yours." After an entire lifetime of denial, my sister was given the name of her father.

> She has her father's eyes, this Bolivian beauty.
> The soil of his ancestry
> Had formed aspects of her life,
> Just as surely and differently
> As my father's formed mine.

Feeling safe doesn't seem to come from having a roof over your head or from remaining in the grove where you were born. Sometimes growing up means becoming a child again, so that you can sink your feet into the solid earth you are planted in, and soak up what fills your soul and anchors you. This then sets you free to be your *self*.

When all you thought you knew and felt
Has been reduced
Through the flames of change and transformation.

Integration

Anchoring the Web of Life

When I was a child we had lots of big ol' spiders on the farm. One of my very earliest memories of Arizona, *before* the farm, was a particular visit to a family friend's house. The "dad" took me outside and showed me what seemed to be a wall covered with granddaddy long legged spiders. As he put his hand into the gathering they scurried and crawled up his arm. He was delighted by my squeals of terror!

Yet, morning sunlight upon a dew-covered web brings tears of joy to my eyes, as it is a personally powerful symbol of my life's journey. Have you ever seen a tiny spider hanging by a single thread of web blowing in the breeze in a seemingly perilous manner? At some point, like that tiny spider, I realized the security that my own thread held. I searched for just the right anchor points to begin to cast a web that would support my healing journey. Perhaps a place in the upper corners of my grandma's kitchen, out of the reach of weekly dusting or spring-cleaning, was where I first anchored as I freefell into my family of origin. It was the place where I associated "safety" and it has remained an unchanging memory and feeling. Like the flow of the web from the sacred place within the spider's body, I feel the ever-present tug at my core when I think of that kitchen. Emotional, spiritual, physical, and mental anchors for the web of my life were what I sought through the fiery years of change and transformation. One by one they each added a component to the web. Yet, not one aspect could stand alone and provide me a fully integrated healing experience.

The majority of my years in psychotherapy offered no real understanding of why a family like ours happens. It gave me labels and descriptions of those generations of secret keepers with eyes refusing to see, learned behaviors, fear and judgment. The results of certain types of abuse and family dysfunction can be seen as predictable. Courses of treatment can be prescribed and an outcome is often defined as success or failure. The real failure, is the inability to identify the core wound of shame. This is not an uncommon occurrence - even today - as it remains an often unspeakable aspect of sexual abuse. The direct approach of my last therapist not only called me to deal with my *Father Shit*, but supported me in naming the core wound. The emotional anchor to my web was formed.

> You can't heal it if you're not willing to look at it
> And own it.

Developing a belief in something beyond this life, unlike what was described to me through Christianity, redefined the foundation of my childhood. It connected me with not only my family grove, but a larger planet and consciousness through the very soil in which our diverse family roots were planted. Mystical experiences revealed a purpose for my birth into this family. *Reason,* not victim, became a keyword to redefining my foundation and early years. Exploring other religions and ancient, spiritual practices introduced me to the belief in reincarnation, which was even part of Christianity's first 400 years of existence. It was *reasonable* to me that a cycle of birth, life, death and rebirth playing out through multiple lifetimes created a completely different perspective for my life. The teachings on the greater cycle prepared the way to release identifying myself as "a victim of incest," and embracing having an experience, heal a wound, and move on. The spiritual anchor to my web was formed.

Riane Eisler's book *Sacred Pleasure* crystallized my awareness of shame and introduced me to the Goddess in her many manifestations. Two women, Nicole Christine and Margaret Starbird, also touched my life in very personal ways guiding me to the Sacred Feminine and Sacred Masculine within.

The first piece of artwork I created flowed into a second which was a self-portrait. Again, I did not understand the image upon completion. *She* was a woman, clearly me, yet dressed from another time. I was holding a skin shawl covered with images and symbols standing upon a hill under a full moon. This portrait journeyed with me to a metaphysical bookstore where the owners looked at the image and said: "Priestess!

There is a woman's circle forming soon that is called a Priestess Process. Here is a book, *Temple of The Living Earth* by the process creatrix Nicole Christine. Read this and see if it calls to you."

Called to me it did, launching a four-year intensive study through The Priestess Process and a one-on-one study with the amazing author, Nicole. She courageously and yet humbly shared her experiences and beliefs through her books, teaching, and modeling of healing what is described as the Madonna/Whore split. Sacred Sexuality was shifted in my consciousness from something lost in lifetimes past, to something present and alive in the world today. Through this course of study I was given new words and put old words into a new context, which reframed my sexual behavior.

If sexuality is sacred, my body is as well.
There is no shame in physically exploring its creation and function.
And, you don't give away or desecrate a *sacred altar*.

Sacred Union was sexual joining partnered with the original intention of a *sacred act*. This not only created children and a blissful experience when entered consciously, but also as Margaret Starbird's work reveals, was an aspect of early Christianity denied by the church fathers for 2000 years. Margaret became the second profound woman of influence when her books, *The Goddess in the Gospel* and *The Woman With the Alabaster Jar*, were recommended to me by Nicole.

Both Nicole and Margaret's work embraced Mary Magdalene as a powerful woman who was the Beloved of Christ. Nicole, who later wrote *Under Her Wings, the Making of a Magdalene*, offered me a perspective of this union, which facilitated another level of my healing. The physical anchor to my web was formed.

Margaret's work, focusing on the marriage of Christ and Magdalene, satisfied my need for a rational, historical explanation of when the Goddess was lost in our current era. Not only that, Margaret showed a path to bring Her back in partnership with God today. Most significantly, it brought me back into relationship with Christ and the gospels of the New Testament. Potentially one of the most significant Christian authors in the current era, Margaret's methodical research focuses solely on the Gospels. Put in historical context, and viewed through the ancient practice of gematria, (a type of numerology) she shares her work on behalf of the restoration of Sacred Union. Approachable and authentic, Margaret became a dear friend over the years. She is a model for sharing what one believes as truth from a passionate and heartfelt, yet rational and nonjudgmental perspective. Her message spoke to that part of me that thrived in the engineering world of rational, logical details – manna for my mind. The mental anchor for my web was formed.

Separately, psychotherapy, spirituality, knowledge of my body, and reason did not offer the fullness of what I needed to shift my world to a place of abundant existence. However, each was a vital aspect of the whole transformation.

Spending years in a therapist's chair simply played with my emotions until I found a true healer who was *to the point* and called me to be responsible for my thoughts, feelings, and actions. This woman guided me as I reached into the core of my gut and pulled out the deepest and darkest pieces to be explored in the light of day.

The church of my youth preached I should leave dealing with sinners to God and my job was to forgive them. This left me powerless and empty. The shift to a belief in an evolving divine presence within, rather than an external God in heaven made me holy. And, if I no longer believed in hell and damnation for myself, I couldn't wish that upon those who had abused me.

Emotional clarity and a spiritual shift could not teach me how to consciously, physically BE in my own body. Treating my body as physically insignificant was an identifiable sign of one who had experienced sexual abuse. Recognizing the value and beauty of my own human form re-dignified my physical being.

And yet, the emotional, spiritual and physical anchors did not address the lingering "but why" questions. They could only be answered to my satisfaction by choosing to study, gaining some knowledge, and developing an understanding of what would be my truth.

Each anchor was an essential piece that supported my transformation and together, they completely reframed the experiences of my life.

> Emotional healing calms the inner waters
> Creating a new flow of love.
> Spiritual healing sparks inspiration
> Creating a new faith and passion.
> Physical healing reforms the vessel
> Creating a new home for BEing.
> Mental healing brings clarity of thought
> Creating a new mind that knows Self.

The web that I wove is ultimately one of personal responsibility and uniquely my own. However, for decades, great thinkers such as Ken Wilber have been exploring the *combination* of eastern and western philosophies to create an integrated healing experience. The timely discovery of books such as Wilbur's *Spectrum of Consciousness* validated my experience. It gave me a feeling of personal satisfaction, and challenged me to stretch and explore even more.

As a visual artist, the images I created during this time of transformation often contributed to sparks of understanding. When I first saw a diagram of the chakra energy system from an ancient Hindu tradition, I was struck by the range of colors that represented the seven centers. Further exploration expanded my understanding that life experiences impact chakras and that healing focused on one, like the anchors of my web, did not heal the whole. When putting my experience into the context of the chakras, I realized that healing the second charka or sexual center without addressing the solar plexus or third charka, where shame resides, moves us forward but does did not fully heal an experience of sexual abuse. I needed to address each and every center. The magic is that in this context I was able to see how the combination of heart stopping moments of awareness and shifts were not isolated but woven throughout my body. This created integrated changes and transformations, healing not only my wounds but also aligning me to be present to the shifts of those closest to me.

I've been called a lot of names, and described in a lot of ways in my life. Certainly *Patty, Pat* and *Patricia* have expressed the wide variety of ways I've looked at myself. Add the multiple last names I've carried through birth, adoption and four marriages, I am a virtual smorgasbord! While some might look at my life and say I'm flighty and don't stick with things - marriages, religions - I now reflect on these changes with deep gratitude for my flexibility and openness. I believe I came into this life with a purpose and my experiences put me in the perfect setting for a total life altering change and transformation. Also, I now believe that at each and every moment, I was in exactly the right place, and I recognize my life as being abundant from the moment I was born.

Certainly, it took tremendous work to get to a place where I was aware that Patricia Kay Ballentine was someone to not only reclaim, but also to hold onto with a deep sense of devotion and passion. Ultimately, the deepest work was to discover who I was at my core, what I was going to choose to believe, and how I would move forward and express in the world. Patricia Kay Ballentine has been my most present and vocal guide, as the voice within screaming from the depths of my pain, or expressing the absolute ecstatic joy at my triumphs.

Integrated…
With the tools of my choosing
That became
The anchors of my web of life…
We are *one*,
And thus,
I *am* Whole!

*You emerge
As the ABUNDANCE
Of YOU!*

In Service

Where Magic Happens

At fifty years of age I found myself a virgin and living completely alone for the first time in my life. Believed by many to be one of the most mistranslated words in the last 2000 years, virgin means *a woman whole and complete unto herself.* This is markedly different than a woman who has never had sexual intercourse with a man. Mistranslation or not, I felt fresh and whole and yet slightly startled when I realized that I was literally living alone for the first time in my life. I had gone from the homes of my parents and grandparents, to marriage and motherhood, being a live-in girlfriend, and finally sharing my older sister's home. The timing was again absolutely perfect, as I stepped into myself in yet one more new way by choosing to live *alone*. Not even a four-legged friend for companionship!

I had become very adept at being with myself. Sometimes I would carve out a corner in a coffee shop garden with my journal at 6:00 a.m. every day for months. Other times would find me heading down the road in my jeep toward an unknown destination. With regularity I separated myself from those I lived, worked, loved or played with. It took practice to develop a habit of creating the physical and emotional space for ME to continue to transform and expand.

> I have spent time with myself when I was
> Extremely happy,
> And when I was deeply sad…
> When I was feeling completely peaceful,
> Absolutely inspired …
> And explosively energetic.

At this turning, instead of carving out time, I was literally living in solitude. This created more shifts, and I stayed aware to insure a balanced life. Being a very active woman with grown sons nearby, a grandbaby, full time job, and an expanding part time ministry, days and evenings were very full. For the first few months of my new life, I still chose to schedule specific amounts of time when I was awake and had energy, to BE with myself, continuing my commitment to inner exploration. It was a life supporting practice and I wanted to completely honor it. The significance of this was revealed through my personal experience, and also the observation of others through my expanding role as a group facilitator and spiritual counselor.

>Solitude is not honored in our culture,
>Yet it is in those moments of truly being one with self…
>That we experience the
>Magnitude of our Oneness with All.

From the childhood memories of my connection to nature, to the late night energetic frenzy of creating that first piece of art, the experience of *being alone* was absolutely essential for transformation. And in those hours I had no feeling of loneliness, but rather an expansive sense of connection to energies unseen but very present that supported my every thought and action. This type of solitude is not the same as the "I'll just put my chin down and get through this challenge by myself" being alone. I've clearly used that as a survival tool in the past. Although I embrace solitude, it's not a place I prefer *over* connecting with others. Rather, for me, it is a part of a fully conscious life that brings balance to my world. It is where I pause to reflect upon and integrate the constant transformation in my life.

In moments of solitude we hear the voice of our soul friend. Sometimes she is the inner child lost decades ago. Sometimes she is the daughter who, in the solitude, is able to reconcile enough experiences with her mother, to be able to see and feel the flash of inspiration, which brings transformation to the relationship.

>I remember feeling lonely…
>And it was almost never
>When I was alone.

Reduced to Abundance

I'm not certain that I can say we learn to embrace solitude first, and then hear the voice within or that it happens the other way around. In my experience, the two seem to flow with each other. I *am* certain that regardless of whether we are doing physical, spiritual, emotional or mental work, the presence of solitude is essential for transformation. Transformation led me to peace.

> The greatest gift I have received
> In this life,
> As I have chosen to live it,
> The one thing that has emerged
> Through the journey
> Of being
> Reduced to Abundance
> Is
> An *abundantly*
> Peaceful presence.

In yet another flash of understanding, I knew I could truly touch peace in my life. The religious expression of "being in a state of grace" was given new meaning for me. My journey to grace however, took me to the center of chaos where I believe creation begins. Chaos, like virgin, is a word whose real meaning and purpose has been buried under layers of negativity. This makes it something many strive to eliminate from their lives, rather than integrate. Yet, in my experience chaos is essential for life altering change and transformation. The challenge was learning to move through my resistance as I was drawn into the swirling energy. I had to learn to be consciously *in* the experience, then move through the spin to the calm center where I could pause, reflect, and receive the transformational flash of awareness.

> Whirling energy of chaos
> Or
> Silence of solitude…
> Which one do we resist or fear more?

Patricia Ballentine

> We can hide from ourselves
> In either.

In the places of our lives where we are least willing to go, we will most likely find what we are truly looking for. Like a portal to the soul, or the inner child, there is a doorway to our healing or transformation. We hold our own keys however, and ultimately choose when (or if) we will open the door and begin the journey. We choose what life stories we are going to explore and what experiences feel the most significant.

We choose what wounds we are going to hold on to and what we will release. We choose whose voice offers wisest counsel, the one within, or those of the world around us. We choose whether or not to hold onto the religions of our past, or to look courageously at the hold they have on us and embark upon a new spiritual path.

During this time I had a wonderful opportunity to meet a therapist, Mary, who shared my belief that something within many therapy processes wasn't working. She and I had been peers in support groups, experiencing the therapy process, getting pieces, but feeling like there were holes. A dynamic web weaver with her own view of anchors, we looked at the fullness of our experiences - our bags of tools - and decided to create a partnership that would offer a more holistic healing experience. The trick was to integrate the emotional, spiritual, physical, and mental components without creating new layers of perceived separation or judgment. Inspired by John O'Donohue's book *Anam Cara: A Celtic Book of Wisdom*, we asked groups of women to make a six-month commitment to explore their deepest issues from the perspective of being their own "Anam Cara" or "Soul Friend."

This book had become one that I traveled with, shared with others most often, and used as a personal touchstone more than any other. A blending of the ancient Celtic or Pagan ways and Christianity, it provides beautiful descriptions of life and experiences that are presentable to people from a wide range of religious or spiritual orientations.

As our tool within the group each week, I would randomly select a passage, reflect, and write a meditation. Then I created an altar that became a physical sign of the message. In group, the passage from the book was read, the meditation and the altar set the framework for the experience that followed. Rather than a specific wound being the focus for each group meeting, what creatively flowed from the random reading set the intention for the evening.

Whether the woman was an incest survivor, living with chronic pain, experiencing depression, or looking for a "meaning" for her life, she was provided a unique environment in which to tell her story. What often emerged was a new perspective. Mary's therapeutic skill brought the tough pieces to the surface within a spiritually transformational and inclusive circle that always involved ceremony, and bodywork if appropriate. We began to see shifts in the lives of women, many of whom had been working on the same pieces for years without feeling they had made progress.

Religious orientations were always given voice and honored. Through the words of philosopher and Catholic Theologian O'Donohue so beautifully expressed in *Anam Cara*, many of the participants were able to see the similarities between the ancient and not so ancient practices. Not only did they see them, but they also had a safe experience of exploring different paths they might choose to embark upon as part of their healing process. Some found new meaning in the orthodox religion of their choosing. Others released their religion as one of the aspects of their lives that no longer served them. Our primary goal within that six-month commitment was for each woman to get a glimpse of herself as the *Anam Cara*. Sometimes the most difficult part of the experiences was learning to simply sit in silence or allowing another to weep without being held or "helped."

> The friend within
> Once found
> Will always be there.
> The friend within
> Once found
> Will become
> The first source
> Of wise counsel…
> Rather than the last.

Service to others took the form of creating and holding space where what I had learned was offered to women who showed up in synchronistic timing. I began each gathering with the words "embrace if you resonate with what I share, release to the Mother Earth if you do not", making it clear that freedom of choice, not projection of beliefs, was fundamental to my service.

The most powerful magic happens inside each of us when we truly understand our power to choose. It begins as a glimpse of what might be, then expands over time until we recognize ourselves through our own eyes. If we have been true to our journey, the day arrives when the magic of transformation cannot be denied, and we understand that it is also, a never ending process.

Epilogue

The Carousel of Life

I have always loved merry-go-rounds. From the smallest two horse variety often seen outside a grocery store to the grandeur of a hand carved and detailed, mechanical musical wonderland; they are identical in the fundamental function – they go 'round and 'round – just like life. And the cycles of life can visit us in a beautiful loving way, or they can be the harbingers of returning experiences that painfully reveal what is yet unresolved.

> Experiences returning
> Like prancing horses
> Moving
> To the melodic tunes of time.
> Will I race to ride
> Then dizzily lose my balance
> And fall from my mount?
> Or will I ride with grace and control
> One with the music and steed….
> Or even…
> Simply stand peacefully
> Watching the painted ponies
> Go 'round and 'round.

I have been keeping journals for many years, chronicling the early rants of a wild woman or capturing the whispers of my artistic muses. Over time I recognized the repetition of experiences. As I began to pay closer attention, I realized there was a definite pattern when similar themes were noted.

I could see that at certain times of the month my emotions seemed stronger – even out of control. As women we often associate this with our hormonal and menstrual cycles. As I became more in touch with the cycles of nature I understood the phases of the moon also impacted my body. Over time and with intention, I shifted my own cycle to align with the waxing and waning lunar energies. My blood flowed at the new moon, and I felt the surge of my own fertility at the full moon. This was an important first step in aligning me with the greater energetic resource of nature. It was also a tremendously empowering shift as I released using the time of the month as an excuse for emotional outbursts, and began to honor the underlying flow of energy that was connected to my emotions.

As I expanded my awareness of the cycles in my life, I could see where seasons and other significant times of the year brought repeated thoughts and feelings. As I began this journey of transformation to abundance I realized that my reaction (or response) to a reoccurring event was never identical to those of others sharing the same experience.

My older sister and I were both born in the same month. My birthday is four days before hers. One of my fondest early birthday memories was coming to Grandma's kitchen table and seeing two identical cakes. They were built around dolls and their beautiful dresses were the cakes, decorated with flowers. The only difference was the color of their garments. It was decades later that I realized how painful the close proximity of our birthdays was to my sister. This was prompted when she was a child and our mother advised that the birthday celebration she so looked forward to the year I was born, was canceled because she had to help "take care of the baby."

By journaling and tracking the dates of events (remarkable and seemingly un-remarkable) I developed an extensive library of self-references. As I became more aware of cycles in nature, tools such as astrological timings, and even unfolding world events, I would add those to my notes. Monthly awareness brought quicker revelations while larger cycles took more time.

"Everything that happens once can never happen again. But everything that happens twice will surely happen a third time."
~ Paulo Coelho, *The Alchemist*

The first year of journaling built a baseline of sorts. As the second year began, I saw patterns forming and gained information with which to work. There were events that were remarkable and never repeated. There were events that repeated numerous times in the course of the year and literally screamed for my immediate attention. And there were events that seemed to build over days or weeks with a clear crescendo exactly a year to the day of when noted in the previous year's journaling.

> The deepest work
> Is that
> Which the larger cycle reveals.
> And the most profound healing
> Is that
> Which the returning cycle affirms.

Journaling, recognizing the patterns, and awareness of my own cycles were powerful keys in the work to be done. I embraced the affirmation of completion when the cycle came 'round one more time, and I felt no energetic charge from the experience. Paulo Coelho's quote identifies a formula. The first cycle reveals the wound, the second reveals the progress of the work, and the third affirms the healing. And indeed, sometimes it takes many returns, perhaps even lifetimes. But the time will surely come when we stand peacefully … watching the painted ponies go by.

> And in that peace
> We know
> We have truly been *Reduced to Abundance*

In the end, many have said to me, "This is so much work. There are easier ways." To this I respond, for me, life is to be lived fully, not necessarily easily. I have created and learned to live a life *Reduced to Abundance*. Choosing this path does not eliminate the relevance of any aspect of my life, but renders the essential essence from each.

It is the good work that empowers me to live the ancient aphorism *Know Thyself*. It is the lifelong work that offers no quick fix, choosing to season my own simmering pot over time, and to ultimately be one with the carousel of my own life. And in what is true for me, it is the soulful work that prepares the way for the ongoing adventure when the carousel ride of this lifetime pauses ... and the next begins.

Made in the USA
San Bernardino, CA
02 June 2015